Brimming with creative inspiration, how-to projects, and useful information to enrich your everyday life, Quarto Knows is a favourite destination for those pursuing their interests and passions. Visit our site and dig deeper with our books into your area of interest: Quarto Creates, Quarto Cooks, Quarto Homes, Quarto Lives, Quarto Drives, Quarto Explores, Quarto Gifts, or Quarto Kids.

ISBN 978-1-78603-179-2 (US)
ISBN 978-1-78603-040-5 (UK)

Illustrated with ink and digital media
Set in Bodoni, Futura BT and CastlePress

Published by Jenny Broom and Rachel Williams
Designed by Karissa Santos
Translated by Polkadot Global Ltd

Manufactured in Dongguan, China, China TL012018
9 8 7 6 5 4 3 2 1

This book belongs to

NAME: -

PASCAL BLANCHET

GO WEST!

AMERICA BY RAILROAD

WIDE EYED EDITIONS

All *aboard!* shouts the guard, as he walks along the platfrom, preparing the train for departure. Trains are made up of wagons, but we say "cars" when we are talking about the kind that carry passengers—so hop inside and take a seat!

With this book you will set off on a journey across the vast continent of North America, from Montreal to Los Angeles, and discover the great cities and breathtaking scenery of these beautiful lands. You will also journey through time, to explore the fascinating story of train travel through history.

So what are you waiting for? Grab your bags and let's begin your journey!

GETTING READY TO LEAVE

Before we leave, remember to have your ticket handy. Here it is!

At every stop, the conductor will punch it to show you which city you're in.

Your ticket shows the cities where the train will stop.

And the logo of the railroad company we're traveling with will be here.

MONTREAL
NEW YORK
BUFFALO
CHICAGO
OMAHA
DENVER
CHEYENNE
COUTTS
CALGARY
BANFF
VANCOUVER
SEATTLE
SAN FRANCISCO
LOS ANGELES

GO WEST!
AMERICA BY RAILROAD

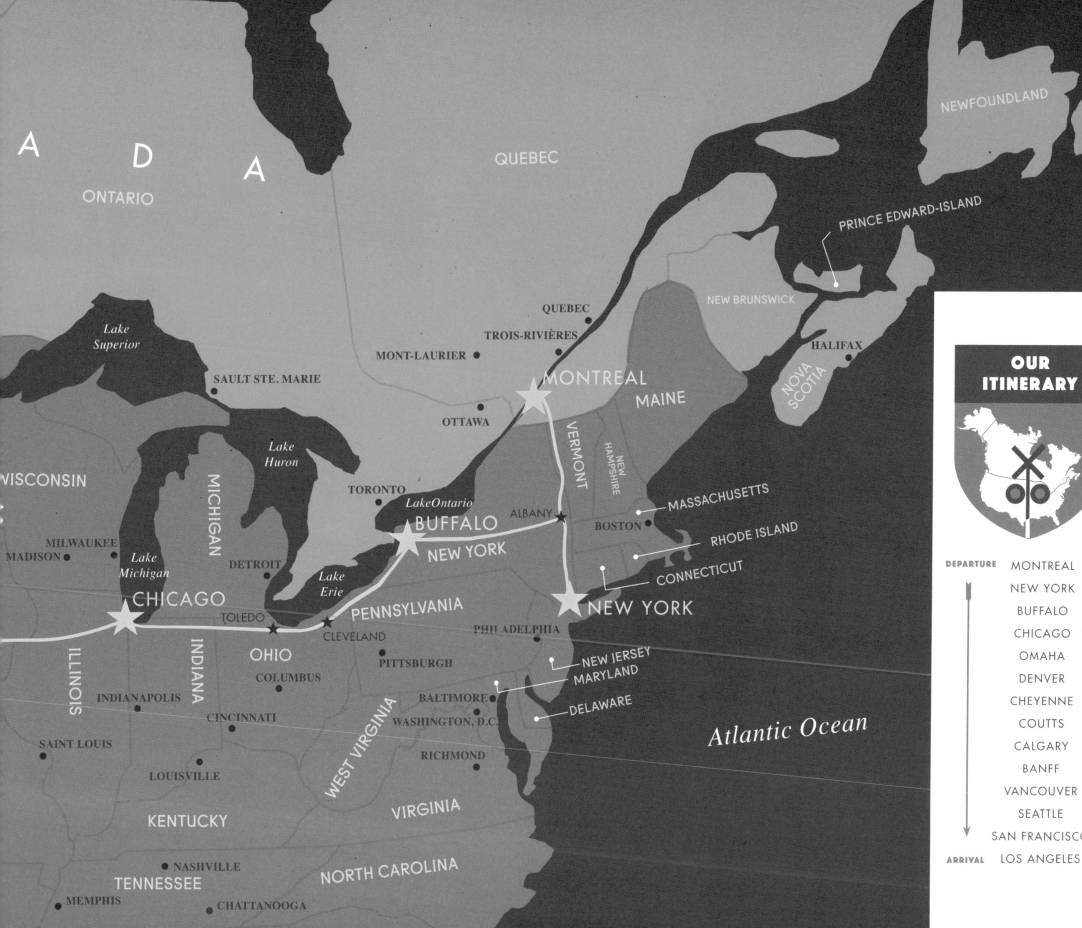

CANADA

ONTARIO

Lake Superior

SAULT STE. MARIE

QUEBEC

Lake Huron

Lake Michigan

MICHIGAN

MONT-LAURIER

QUEBEC

TROIS-RIVIÈRES

OTTAWA

MONTREAL

NEWFOUNDLAND

PRINCE EDWARD-ISLAND

NEW BRUNSWICK

HALIFAX

NOVA SCOTIA

MAINE

VERMONT

NEW HAMPSHIRE

MASSACHUSETTS

BOSTON

RHODE ISLAND

CONNECTICUT

TORONTO

WISCONSIN

MILWAUKEE

MADISON

DETROIT

TOLEDO

Lake Ontario

BUFFALO

NEW YORK

ALBANY

Lake Erie

CHICAGO

ILLINOIS

INDIANA

OHIO

Lake Michigan

PENNSYLVANIA

CLEVELAND

PHILADELPHIA

NEW YORK

NEW JERSEY

MARYLAND

DELAWARE

Atlantic Ocean

INDIANAPOLIS

COLUMBUS

PITTSBURGH

CINCINNATI

SAINT LOUIS

WEST VIRGINIA

BALTIMORE

WASHINGTON, D.C.

LOUISVILLE

RICHMOND

KENTUCKY

VIRGINIA

NASHVILLE

TENNESSEE

NORTH CAROLINA

MEMPHIS

CHATTANOOGA

OUR ITINERARY

DEPARTURE

MONTREAL
NEW YORK
BUFFALO
CHICAGO
OMAHA
DENVER
CHEYENNE
COUTTS
CALGARY
BANFF
VANCOUVER
SEATTLE
SAN FRANCISCO

ARRIVAL   LOS ANGELES

1830

PETER COOPER'S "TOM THUMB

TOM THUMB

In 1830, the first locomotive built in America set out on its maiden journey. It was nicknamed "Tom Thumb" because of its size. It marked the start of rail history in North America and of passenger travel across our great continent.

BO BALTIMORE & OHIO R.R.

THE DORCHESTER LOCOMOTIVE

MONTREAL
NEW YORK
BUFFALO
CHICAGO
OMAHA
DENVER
CHEYENNE
COUTTS
CALGARY
BANFF
VANCOUVER
SEATTLE
SAN FRANCISCO
LOS ANGELES

It's July 1836 and we're starting our journey in Montreal on Canada's very first railroad. A tiny steam locomotive is pulling two carriages of dignitaries the short distance between La Prairie on the St. Lawrence River and St. John on the Richelieu River.

Built in Great Britain and bank-rolled by Montreal brewer, John Molson, the **Dorchester** will provide a faster ride from Montreal to Lake Champlain en route to New York, and spark a new fashion in freight and passenger transport in the country, and beyond.

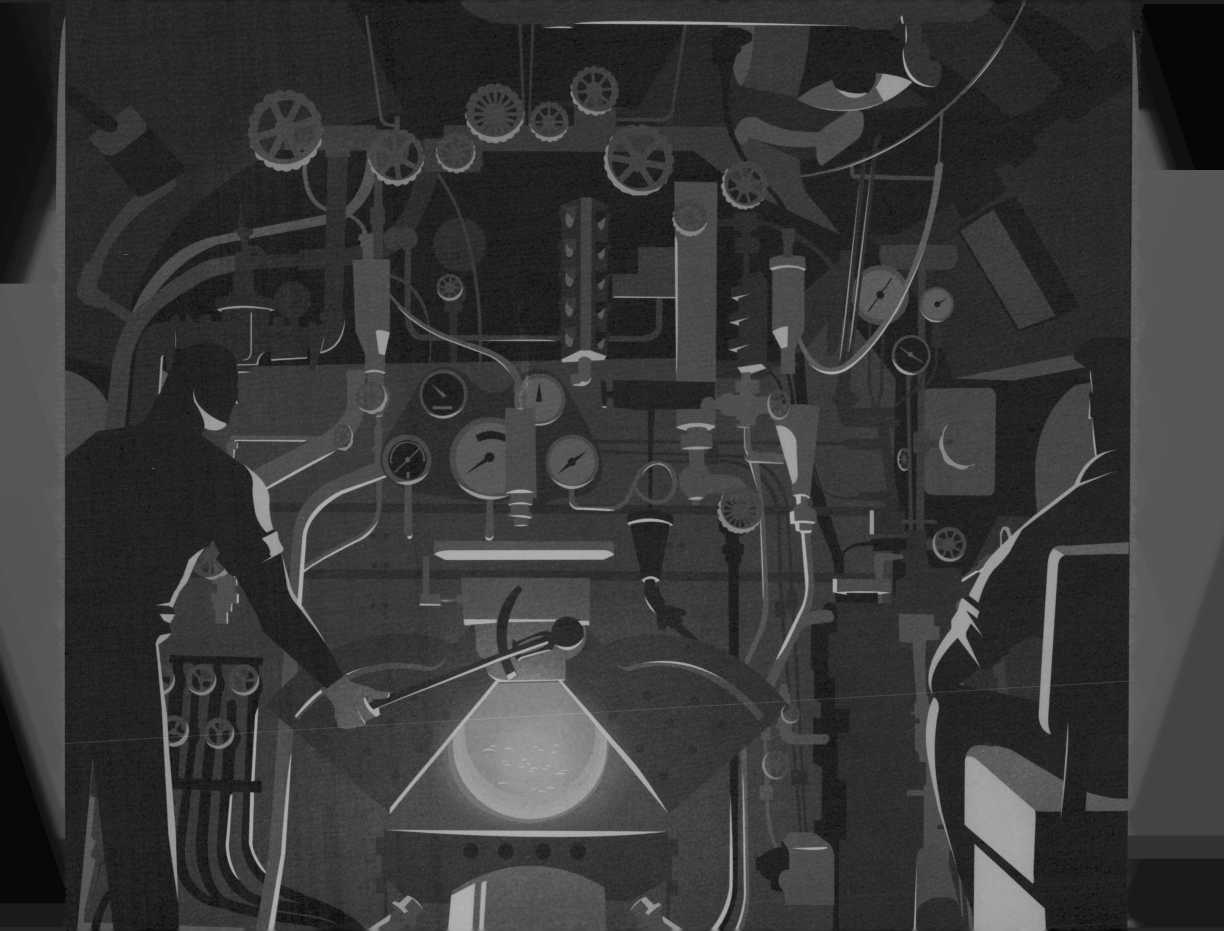

THE FIREMAN AND THE ENGINEER

In the one hundred years following the **Dorchester**'s trip in 1836, steam trains became bigger and more complicated to run. It took two people to keep the train moving: the fireman and the engineer. The fireman's job was to feed the fire and control steam production, while the engineer was the official driver and train manager.

The **T1** locomotive, whose engine room you see here, was built in 1942 for the Pennsylvania Railroad. It was incredibly fast—said to reach speeds of up to 140 miles an hour!

How it happened . . .

BANNERMAN'S CASTLE

En route from Montreal to New York, the railroad runs alongside the Hudson River. The remains of a giant castle lie in the middle of the river, perched on top of a small island. The island is Pollepel, and those are the ruins of Bannerman's Castle.

Built in 1901 by arms dealer Francis (Frank) Bannerman VI, the castle was his family's summer residence as well as a huge arms and munitions warehouse.

Most of the castle was destroyed in 1920, when more than two hundred tons of shells and gunpowder exploded!

NEW YORK CITY

MONTREAL
NEW YORK
BUFFALO
CHICAGO
OMAHA
DENVER
CHEYENNE
COUTTS
CALGARY
BANFF
VANCOUVER
SEATTLE
SAN FRANCISCO
LOS ANGELES

NEW YORK
CENTRAL
SYSTEM

THE CITY THAT NEVER SLEEPS

Welcome to midtown Manhattan. New York is a city of extremes, heart of the American dream, symbol of an entire continent! This city is awake 24/7, buzzing to the beat of Broadway shows, and home to Wall Street, one of the world's largest financial districts. New York City is also home to one of America's busiest railroad stations—Grand Central Terminal.

Grand Central Terminal opened its doors in 1871, but was soon demolished and replaced by a much grander building. Then, on February 2, 1913, more than 150,000 wide-eyed visitors came to watch the first train–the **Boston Express No. 2**–depart from the new station, at just after midnight.

Speed forward to the 21st century, and the station has 44 platforms and 67 tracks–covering an area underground of 48 acres, from 42nd to 49th street. It is estimated that more than 750,000 people pass through this majestic station every day.

The statue you see outside, at the front of the station, is of Cornelius Vanderbilt, nicknamed the "Commodore." He was the billionaire businessman who built Grand Central Terminal. Some people even claim that he invented potato chips, too!

THE FIREGUARD

THE ROOF

THE BELL

THE HEADLAMP

THE COWCATCHER

How it happened . . .

THE AMERICAN LOCOMOTIVE

From the mid-19th century, the railroad's conquest of the continent brought new challenges for train manufacturers.

The American-type steam locomotive was the first one specially designed to work in North America. It had a bell to warn people it was coming, a powerful headlamp for night journeys, and a roof to shelter the fireman and engineer during heavy snowfall and overnight travel. There was also a fireguard to protect the surrounding countryside from any embers flying out of the smokestack, and a cowcatcher to push any obstacles off the tracks.

On your left, you can see the **Jupiter** locomotive, built in 1868. It's one of the most famous of the American-type locomotives.

Stop 3
BUFFALO CENTRAL TERMINAL

Here we are at Buffalo—halfway between New York and Chicago—in 1929, just in time to visit the newly opened Central Terminal. It is one of the most beautiful art deco buildings in the U.S.A., with an enormous arched waiting hall, restaurant and soda fountain, a seventeen-story office tower, and its own power station!

Sadly, in fifty years' time—as passenger train travel gradually declines—the station will lose its appeal, and the last train will leave Buffalo Central Terminal at 4:10am on October 28, 1979. The station doors may close, but its glory days will never be forgotten.

- MONTREAL
- NEW YORK
- BUFFALO
- CHICAGO
- OMAHA
- DENVER
- CHEYENNE
- COUTTS
- CALGARY
- BANFF
- VANCOUVER
- SEATTLE
- SAN FRANCISCO
- LOS ANGELES

NEW YORK CENTRAL SYSTEM

How it happened . . .

THE RED CARPET

At 6pm Eastern Time on June 15, 1938, the newly streamlined **20th Century Limited** left Grand Central Terminal in New York, for its maiden journey on the New York–Chicago line, stopping at Buffalo en route.

The train was like something from a Hollywood movie. Every passenger was treated like a star, walking along a red carpet to board the train. The tradition of walking along a red carpet at galas and important events began here.

Created by industrial designer Henry Dreyfuss, this train embodied the luxury, comfort, and modernity of the time.

In the 1860s, railway companies began to take an interest in travelers' comfort. More and more passengers wanted comfortable cars where they could eat and sleep. George Pullman seized the opportunity and founded the Pullman Palace Car Company in 1867. His company specialized in building passenger cars. Other companies followed suit, provoking feverish competition in luxury train travel.

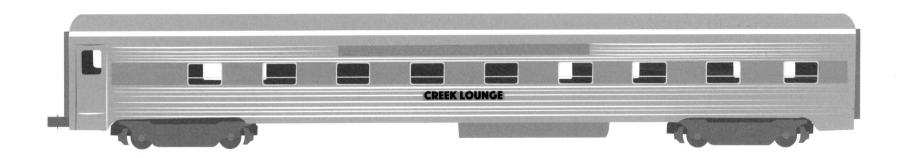

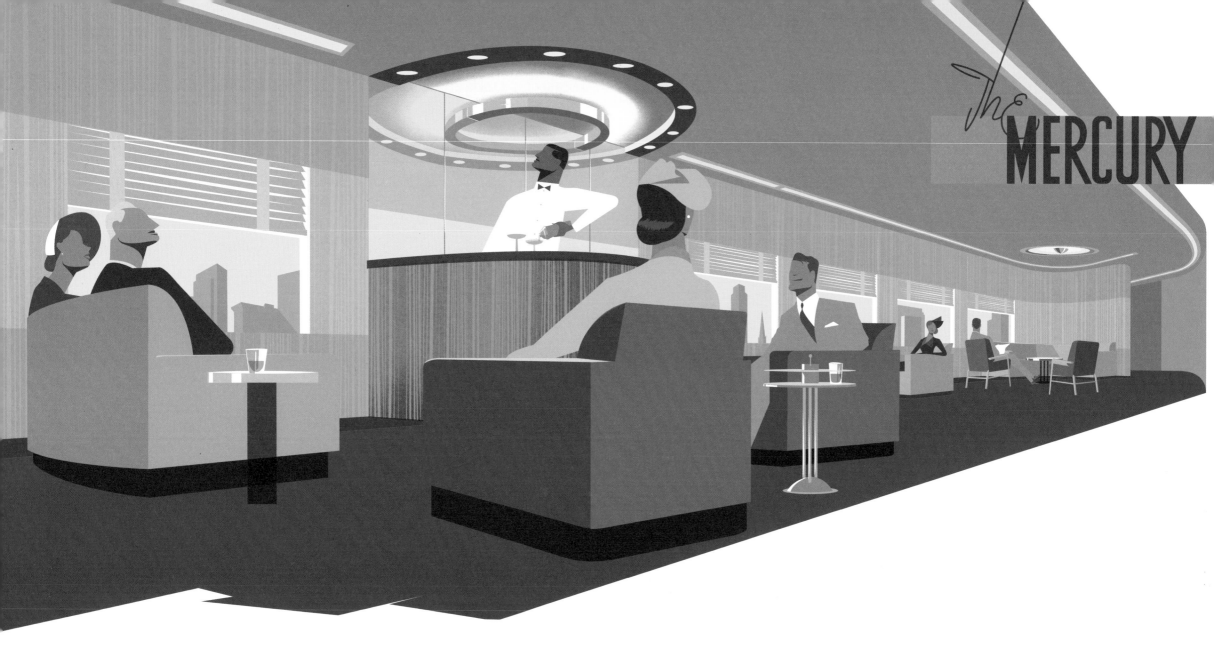

THE LOUNGE CAR

Settled in a soft armchair, you could enjoy a chocolate, vanilla, or strawberry milkshake while you watched the scenery go by and chatted to other passengers, or read the morning newspapers. In the lounge car, with its exotic wood veneers and gleaming chrome, you could travel in style at more than 60 miles per hour.

THE DINING CAR

On the menu: Chicken Maryland, Western Prime Rib, Camembert on Toast, and Peaches and Cream. The dining car had a chef, cooks, and elegant waiters serving the train passengers. Its polished silverware and brilliant white tablecloths offered five-star dining at its finest.

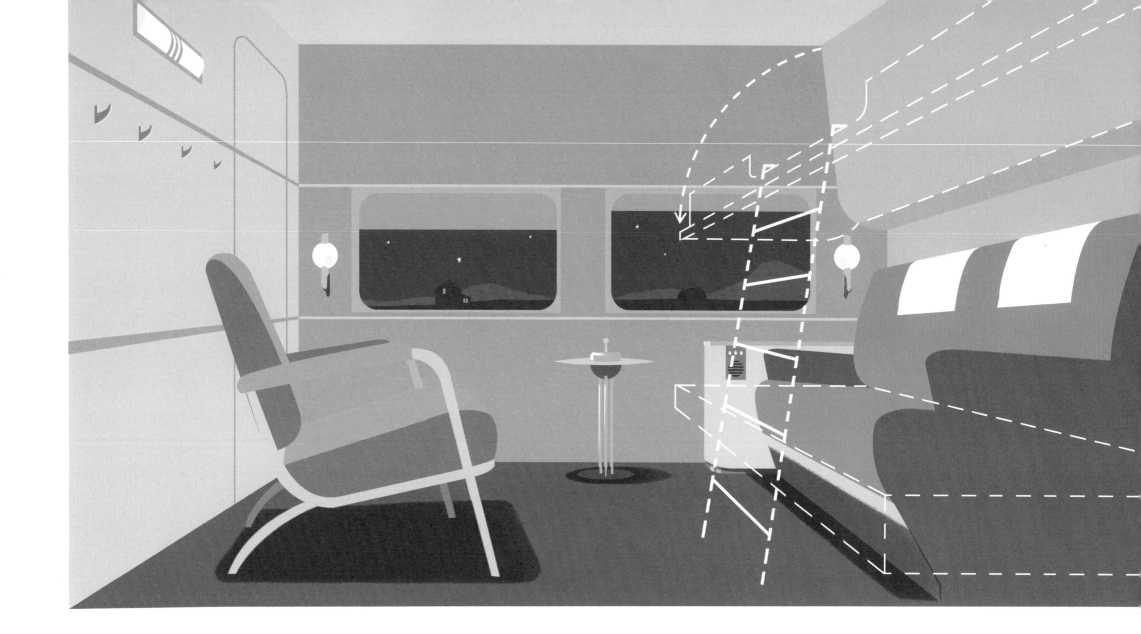

THE SLEEPER

Long distance travel saw the arrival of "sleeper trains." Luxury compartments had wide seats, reading lights, a toilet cubicle, and a closet. In the evening, a porter would unfold the seat and open the panel above, creating two comfortable beds where passengers could drift off to sleep to the gentle motion of the train.

Rear car/observation lounge

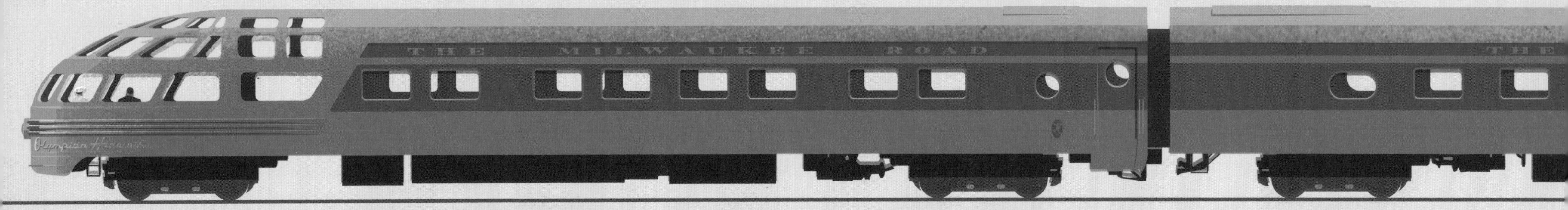

Passenger car

Dining car

"Dome car"

ILWAUKEE ROAD

THE MILWAUKEE ROAD

CANADIAN PACIFIC

CANADIAN

Here are a few other famous passenger trains from last century: the **Olympian Hiawatha**, the **Canadian Pacific**, and the **20th Century Limited**.

The
CLASS A

THE
MILWAUKEE
ROAD

THE *Olympian Hiawatha*

Built in 1935, the Milwaukee Road steam **Class A** locomotive pulled the **Olympian Hiawatha** luxury train. Created by the renowned designer Otto Kuhler, it was the first locomotive in history to exceed 112 miles per hour.

The ROYAL HUDSON

The TURBO TRAIN

How it happened . . .

THE LEGENDS

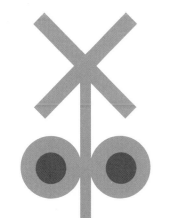

One of the most beautiful and legendary locomotives in North America was the Canadian Pacific's **Hudson** steam engine, built at the Montreal Locomotive Works in 1938. The Hudson acquired its "Royal" title the following year, when it pulled the train carrying King George VI of Great Britain during his visit to Canada. Another awe-inspiring locomotive was the futuristic **Turbo Train**, launched in 1968 and designed by the United Aircraft Corporation. The "Turbo" really lived up to its name, reaching speeds of up to 140 miles per hour!

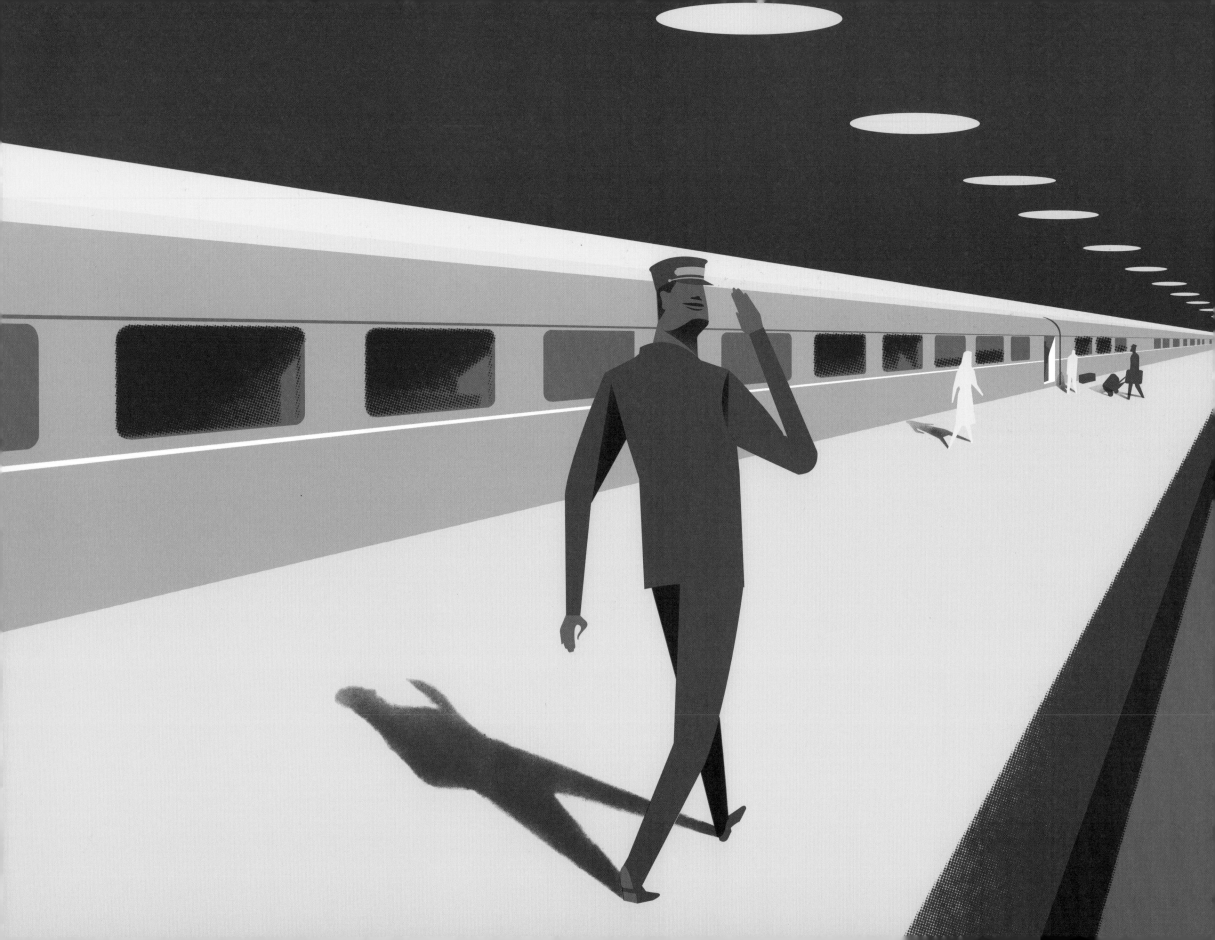

After the Civil War ended in 1865, the Pullman Company hired freed slaves to work on their trains. These employees were known as "Pullman Porters." They faced very difficult working conditions, carrying out tedious and tiring tasks during long working days, with only short breaks. Luxury passenger trains back then were like hotels on wheels. The Pullman Porters were famed for the service, courtesy, and elegance they brought to the great American railroads.

In 1925, Asa Philip Randolph created the first African-American labor union in the United States, to improve working conditions for the Pullman Porters. This marked the beginning of the civil rights movement, and the fight against racial segregation in America.

MONTREAL
NEW YORK
BUFFALO
CHICAGO
OMAHA
DENVER
CHEYENNE
COUTTS
CALGARY
BANFF
VANCOUVER
SEATTLE
SAN FRANCISCO
LOS ANGELES

NEW YORK
CENTRAL
SYSTEM

Here we are at our next stop: Chicago! Nicknamed "The Windy City," it is one of the largest cities in the U.S.A. and sits on the shore of Lake Michigan, one of the five Great Lakes–the biggest group of inland lakes on Earth.

Chicago's many skyscrapers, its industrial power, and legendary jazz music have really captured people's imaginations. From 1900, the city has been dominated by two major league baseball teams: the Cubs and the Whitesox; while the 1920s saw infamous gangster Al Capone fighting rival gangs to be "top dog" during the Prohibition.

How it happened . . .
JAZZ ROUTE

Musicians arriving in Chicago from New Orleans would travel by train, via LaSalle Street Station. After the 1920s, jazz came to symbolize the city. The great artists who performed there include trumpet player Louis Armstrong and cornet player Bix Beiderbecke. Legend has it that on foggy nights, you can still hear Beiderbecke's cornet playing along the shores of Lake Michigan.

How it happened . . .

WEST: THE NEW FRONTIER

n the 1800s, Canada and the United States embarked on one of the most daunting adventures in North American history: to colonize the Wild West.

Until then, only the East of the country had been settled by Europeans, while the West remained unexplored. Between 1840 and 1860, more than 300,000 Americans traveled the 2,000 miles to California, seeking a better life on the Pacific coast. The journey took nearly four months, in canvas-covered wagons drawn by oxen.

Fortunately, construction of the transcontinental railroad across from East to West in the 1860s shortened the trip to just one week.

Stop 5
OMAHA: EAST MEETS WEST

Burlington Route

Welcome to our next stop—Omaha, the largest city in Nebraska!

Construction began from here in 1863 to connect the East and West of the United States by rail. Another team began building from the other end of the line in Sacramento, California, at the same time. Then, on May 10, 1869, two trains full of dignitaries arrived at Promontory Summit, Utah—the point where the final railway spike would be driven in—to mark the opening of the first transcontinental railroad in the U.S.A.

The picture opposite shows the historic handshake between Samuel S. Montague (left) and Grenville M. Dodge (right)—the two chief engineers, respectively in charge of the Central Pacific and the Union Pacific Railroad teams.

How it happened . . .
THE BLACK HILLS BANDITS

On the way from Omaha to our next stop, Denver, we pass Big Springs in Nebraska. This is where, on the night of September 18, 1877, the biggest train robbery in the history of the Union Pacific Railroad took place. Outlaw Sam Bass and his gang, known as the Black Hills Bandits, held up a passing train and stole $60,000 in gold coins—the equivalent of $1.5 million today! This robbery, as well as countless stagecoach robberies beforehand, made Sam Bass one of the most "wanted" men of the American Wild West.

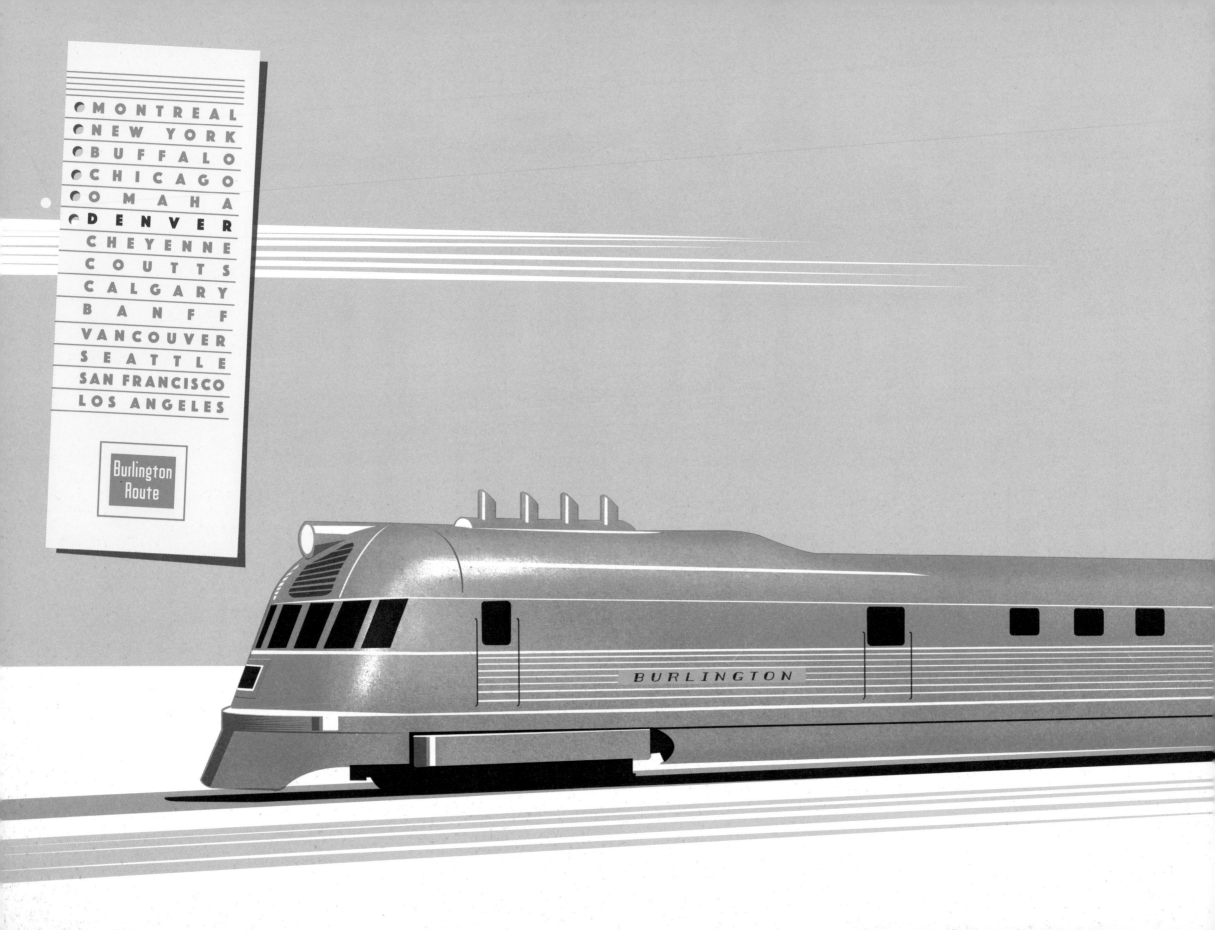

Welcome to Denver, the capital city of the state of Colorado and the highest major city in the U.S.A.—exactly one mile above sea level.

The train linking Chicago to Denver looks straight out of the future, but it actually began operating in 1934. The **Zephyr** was America's first aerodynamic train, pulled by the first ever diesel engine. Its shiny, stainless steel bodywork was lighter and faster than other trains, earning it the nickname the "Silver Streak."

Stop 7

CHEYENNE AND THE IRON HORSE

MONTREAL
NEW YORK
BUFFALO
CHICAGO
OMAHA
DENVER
CHEYENNE
COUTTS
CALGARY
BANFF
VANCOUVER
SEATTLE
SAN FRANCISCO
LOS ANGELES

UNION
PACIFIC

Our next stop, Cheyenne, is home to—and named after—one of the largest Native American peoples on the continent.

They shared the land with the Lakota (a Sioux tribe) and the Arapaho. These Plains Indians hunted the bison for food—there were more than ten million on these plains at the advent of U.S. rail travel.

The arrival of the railroad and the white man brought constant conflict. The pioneers pushed back the First Nations to build the transcontinental railroad, and also killed nearly every bison in North America, leaving the tribespeople starving and destitute.

"Iron Horses" was the name the Cheyenne gave the first trains.

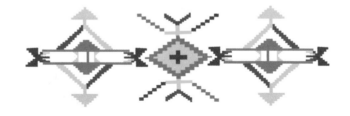

- MONTREAL
- NEW YORK
- BUFFALO
- CHICAGO
- OMAHA
- DENVER
- CHEYENNE
- COUTTS
- CALGARY
- BANFF
- VANCOUVER
- SEATTLE
- SAN FRANCISCO
- LOS ANGELES

Canadian Pacific

Here we are at our next stop already: the border village of Coutts, Alberta!

Built in 1890, this station served as a customs post between the United States and Canada. A line was even painted across the floor of the station dining room to mark the border between the two countries.

Legend has it that a man being hunted by U.S. customs officials calmly crossed the border line into the Canadian part of the station. The customs agents were not allowed to follow him, and could only watch as the fugitive ate his meal.

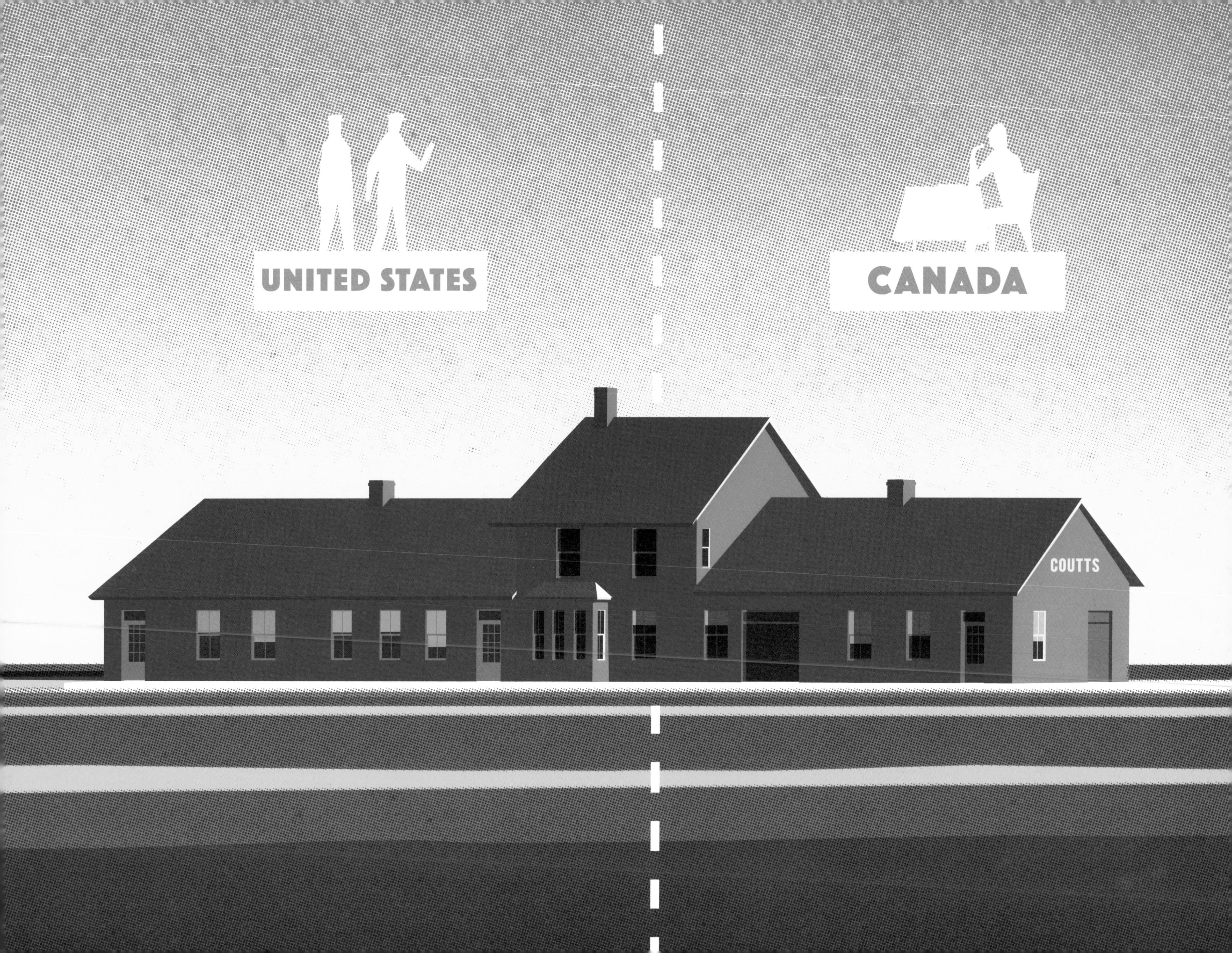

UNITED STATES

CANADA

COUTTS

How it happened . . .
THE LETHBRIDGE VIADUCT

The Lethbridge Viaduct was built between 1907 and 1909 by Montreal's Canadian Pacific Railway. This huge steel trestle bridge spans the Oldman River, and at 2,047 feet long and 311 feet high, it's one of the biggest railway bridges in Canada.

And what's more incredible is that it's still in use today, after more than 100 years of service!

Stop 9
OCEAN TO OCEAN: CALGARY

MONTREAL
NEW YORK
BUFFALO
CHICAGO
OMAHA
DENVER
CHEYENNE
COUTTS
CALGARY
BANFF
VANCOUVER
SEATTLE
SAN FRANCISCO
LOS ANGELES

Here's Calgary—we're more than halfway through our journey already!

It was the Canadian transcontinental railroad that opened up Canada's western provinces—Manitoba, Saskatchewan, Alberta, and British Columbia. In November 1885, the whole country celebrated as the last rail was laid in Craigellachie, British Columbia. Canada was finally connected by rail from the Atlantic to the Pacific Oceans.

It took thousands of men to build the Canadian transcontinental railroad. Among them were Chinese migrants, employed as cheap labor, who worked in extremely dangerous conditions.

In those days, the trip was more like an expedition, and many passengers arrived days late, using an avalanche as their excuse!

THE GRAND RAILROAD HOTELS: BANFF

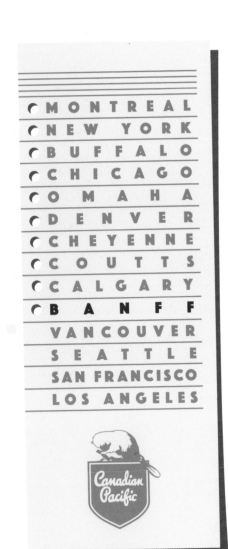

MONTREAL
NEW YORK
BUFFALO
CHICAGO
OMAHA
DENVER
CHEYENNE
COUTTS
CALGARY
BANFF
VANCOUVER
SEATTLE
SAN FRANCISCO
LOS ANGELES

Canadian Pacific

High up in the magnificent Canadian Rocky Mountains, a grand hotel lies nestled among Douglas Fir trees, shrouded in snow.

It is one of the most spectacular Canadian Pacific Railroad hotels: the Banff Springs Hotel. Built in 1888, it has seen many rich and famous visitors over the years: Winston Churchill, the former British Prime Minister, sat comfortably on an Adirondack Chair to smoke his legendary cigars there in 1929; and actress Marilyn Monroe practiced her golf swing on the lawn in 1953 after twisting her ankle during filming.

As the railway companies saw the potential for tourism in these extraordinary landscapes, luxury hotels began popping up all across the continent, and the tourist industry was born.

VANCOUVER, THE NEON CITY

MONTREAL
NEW YORK
BUFFALO
CHICAGO
OMAHA
DENVER
CHEYENNE
COUTTS
CALGARY
BANFF
VANCOUVER
SEATTLE
SAN FRANCISCO
LOS ANGELES

Canadian Pacific

Vancouver, the last stop on the Canadian transcontinental railroad, is a major port on the Pacific Ocean. It is one of Canada's most cosmopolitan cities and 86 percent of its immigrant population are of Asian origin. Vancouver is also famous for its outdoor beauty, with its magnificent parks and many wildlife reserves.

In the mid-1920s, neon signs took over in Vancouver, soon appearing in restaurants, bars, bowling alleys, and even at the train station. By 1953, there were over 19,000 signs—one sign for every 18 inhabitants. After a ban on neon signs for decades, they are back again, lighting up the city's streets.

It's time to head south to our next stop: Seattle! *All aboard!*

Stop 12

MOUNT RAINIER, SEATTLE

Welcome to Seattle! Let's take this opportunity to admire the largest volcano in the United States: Mount Rainier.

Part of the Cascade Range, this huge mountain is nearly three million years old and rises 14,411 feet above sea level. It's not exactly a sleeping giant, either—it's still an active volcano, which geologists monitor closely. The peak of Mount Rainier has the largest amount of permanent snow in the United States!

MONTREAL
NEW YORK
BUFFALO
CHICAGO
OMAHA
DENVER
CHEYENNE
COUTTS
CALGARY
BANFF
VANCOUVER
SEATTLE
SAN FRANCISCO
LOS ANGELES

Here we are in San Francisco, California—the second from last stop on our exciting journey! This is a city of steep, hilly streets, with beautiful painted Victorian houses. Cable cars—the city's trams—rumble past, full of passengers.

San Francisco is also home to one of the seven wonders of the modern world: the Golden Gate Bridge. Opened to traffic in 1937, it is one of the world's longest suspension bridges. It links San Francisco to the city of Sausalito and is painted "international orange," a color that comes from using a special paint to stop the bridge going rusty. Originally, the color was only supposed to be temporary, but it was decided to keep it because people could see the bridge from far away, even through the city's frequent heavy fogs.

In 1937, Southern Pacific Railroads' new, aerodynamic express train, the **Daylight Limited,** began running between San Francisco and Los Angeles. The train took passengers on the scenic Pacific coast route, with the ocean on one side and the sun-drenched Californian landscape on the other.

Advertised as "the most beautiful train in the world," it was easily recognized by its bright red, orange, and black color-scheme. Pulled by the powerful **GS-2** steam locomotive, it was also very fast—making the journey in under 10 hours. The train remained in service until 1974.

Daylight
L I M I T E D

LOS ANGELES UNION STATION

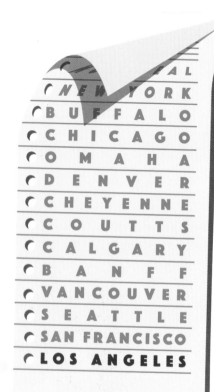

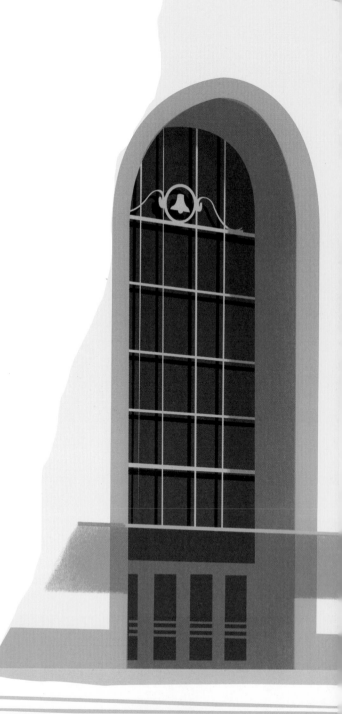

We've arrived at our final destination: Los Angeles. Built in 1939, Union Station is one of the most beautiful stations in the United States, with a tower and tiled roofs that perfectly reflect the west coast's Spanish roots.

Los Angeles, the city of angels, is considered the birthplace of cinema, where Charlie Chaplin made his first films, and where movie stars crowd into the Chinese Theatre each year for the Academy Awards Ceremony. Los Angeles, with its mountains, deserts, and legends, continues to fascinate and inspire people.

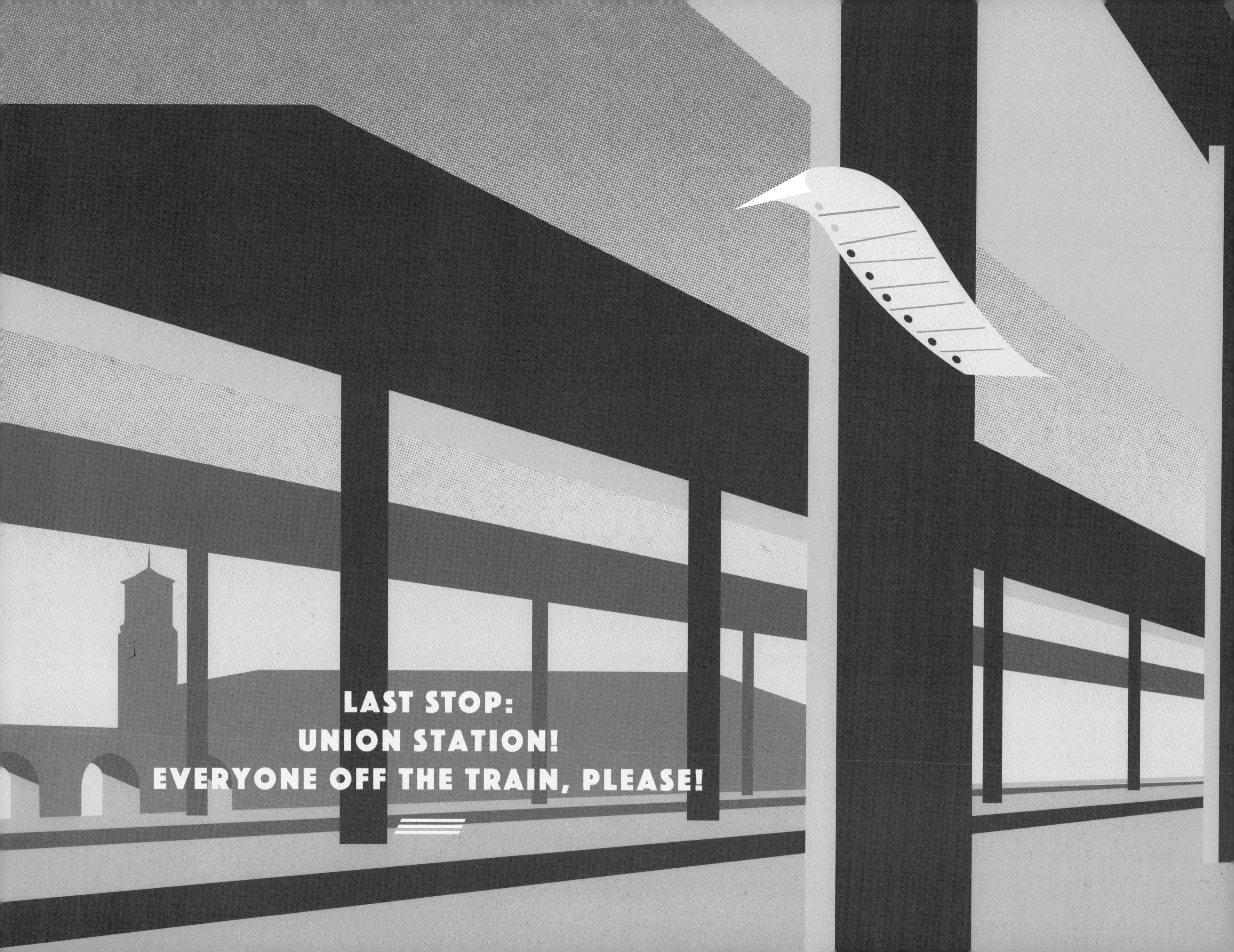

LAST STOP:
UNION STATION!
EVERYONE OFF THE TRAIN, PLEASE!

Our trip west across the North American continent by rail has come to an end.

It's been a pleasure traveling with you!

THE END

SEARCH and FIND

- ○ A fisherman
- ○ An Adirondack chair
- ○ A barrel
- ○ An open book
- ○ 3 clocks
- ○ A cooking pot
- ○ 2 bison
- ○ 2 suitcases
- ○ A beaver

- A double-decker bus ○
- 5 sailboats ○
- An automobile ○
- A cruise ship ○
- A cactus ○
- 4 taxicabs ○
- 3 bow ties ○
- A banjo ○
- A vase of flowers ○